ID0880959

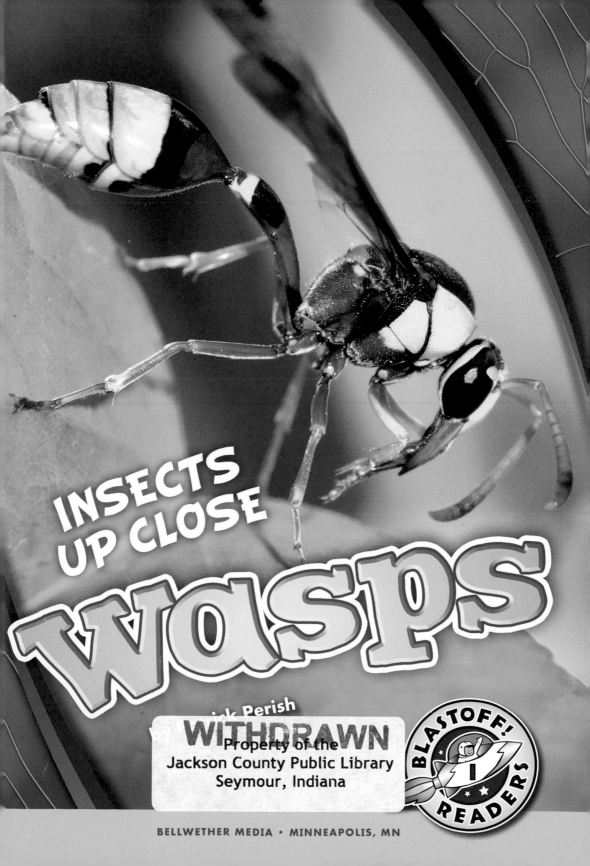

INSECTS UP CLOSE

wasps

by Patrick Perish

BLASTOFF! READERS

BELLWETHER MEDIA • MINNEAPOLIS, MN

Note to Librarians, Teachers, and Parents:

Blastoff! Readers are carefully developed by literacy experts and combine standards-based content with developmentally appropriate text.

Level 1 provides the most support through repetition of high-frequency words, light text, predictable sentence patterns, and strong visual support.

Level 2 offers early readers a bit more challenge through varied simple sentences, increased text load, and less repetition of high-frequency words.

Level 3 advances early-fluent readers toward fluency through increased text and concept load, less reliance on visuals, longer sentences, and more literary language.

Level 4 builds reading stamina by providing more text per page, increased use of punctuation, greater variation in sentence patterns, and increasingly challenging vocabulary.

Level 5 encourages children to move from "learning to read" to "reading to learn" by providing even more text, varied writing styles, and less familiar topics.

Whichever book is right for your reader, Blastoff! Readers are the perfect books to build confidence and encourage a love of reading that will last a lifetime!

This edition first published in 2018 by Bellwether Media, Inc.

No part of this publication may be reproduced in whole or in part without written permission of the publisher. For information regarding permission, write to Bellwether Media, Inc., Attention: Permissions Department, 5357 Penn Avenue South, Minneapolis, MN 55419.

Library of Congress Cataloging-in-Publication Data

Names: Perish, Patrick.
Title: Wasps / by Patrick Perish.
Description: Minneapolis, MN : Bellwether Media, Inc., 2018. | Series: Blastoff! Readers. Insects Up Close | Audience: Age 5-8. | Audience: K to grade 3. | Includes bibliographical references and index.
Identifiers: LCCN 2016057453 (print) | LCCN 2017007901 (ebook) | ISBN 9781626176683 (hardcover : alk. paper) | ISBN 9781681033983 (ebook)
Subjects: LCSH: Wasps–Juvenile literature.
Classification: LCC QL565.2 .P47 2018 (print) | LCC QL565.2 (ebook) | DDC 595.79–dc23
LC record available at https://lccn.loc.gov/2016057453

Editor: Christina Leighton   Designer: Maggie Rosier

Printed in the United States of America, North Mankato, MN.

Table of Contents

What Are Wasps?

Wasps are great hunters. Many of these insects have sharp **stingers**.

stinger

Wasps have thin waists. They are smooth with very few hairs.

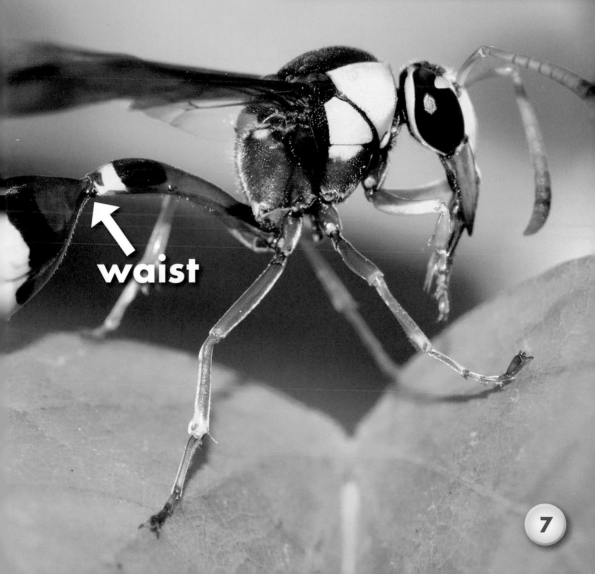

waist

Wasps have bright colors to tell others to stay away. Their bodies may also be shiny!

ruby-tailed
wasp

Living and Eating

Wasps live in trees or ground holes. Some build **paper nests**.

paper nest

Many wasps live in large **colonies**. Others live alone.

colony

Adult wasps often eat **nectar**. They also hunt other insects to feed to their young.

adult
wasp

nectar

15

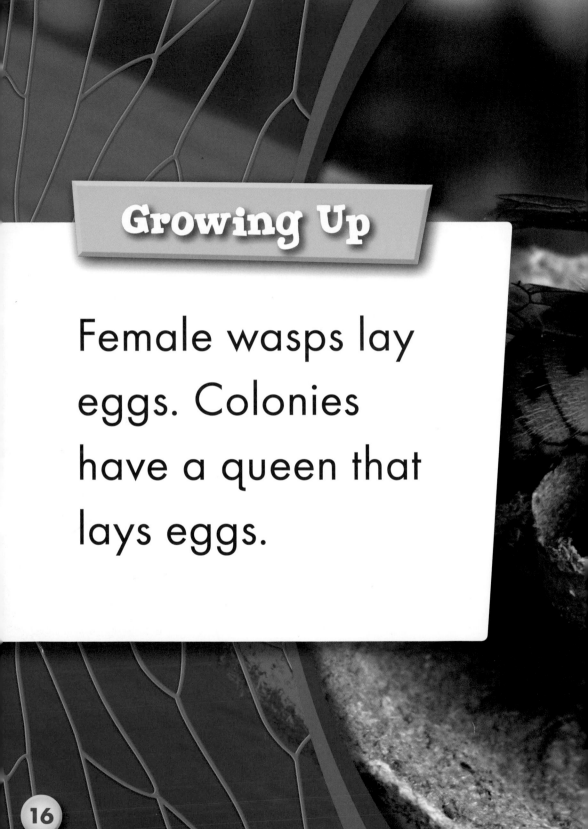

Growing Up

Female wasps lay eggs. Colonies have a queen that lays eggs.

queen

eggs

17

A **larva** comes
from an egg. The
larva grows fast and
becomes a **pupa**.

larvae

pupae

The pupa changes inside a hiding place. It breaks out with wings. Time to fly!

Glossary

colonies

large groups of wasps that work together to live

paper nests

nests made out of plant matter that feels like paper

larva

a baby insect that has come from an egg

pupa

a young insect that is about to become an adult

nectar

a sweet liquid that comes from plants, especially flowers

stingers

sharp body parts that can release a harmful liquid called venom

To Learn More

AT THE LIBRARY

Rockwood, Leigh. *Tell Me the Difference Between a Bee and a Wasp.* New York, N.Y.: PowerKids Press, 2013.

Scarborough, Kate, and Martin Camm. *A Wasp Builds a Nest: See Inside a Paper Wasp's Nest and Watch It Grow.* Richmond Hill, Ont.: Firefly Books, 2016.

Schuh, Mari. *Wasps.* Minneapolis, Minn.: Bullfrog Books, 2015.

ON THE WEB

Learning more about wasps is as easy as 1, 2, 3.

1. Go to www.factsurfer.com.

2. Enter "wasps" into the search box.

3. Click the "Surf" button and you will see a list of related web sites.

With factsurfer.com, finding more information is just a click away.

Index

The images in this book are reproduced through the courtesy of: Kumchai, front cover, pp. 6-7; Pavel Krasensky, pp. 4-5; Cornel Constantin, pp. 5, 22 (bottom right); BIOSPHOTO/ Alamy, pp. 8-9; sasagogaa, pp. 10-11; luismiguelij, pp. 12-13, 22 (top left); Lee Dalton/ Alamy, pp. 14-15; Srijira Ruechapaisarnanak, pp. 15, 22 (bottom left); blickwinkel/ Alamy, pp. 16-17; AmyLv, pp. 18-19; NHPA/ Photoshot / SuperStock, pp. 19 (left), 22 (center left); Esa Hiltula/ age fotostock/ SuperStock, pp. 19 (right), 22 (center right); NattapolStudiO, pp. 20-21; FCG, p. 22 (top right).